A Young E
Book 12: Angry Kids!

Written By: David M. Smith

Copyright

The "A Young Boy Named David" series is owned by Kingdom Being Consultants, LLC. No part of this publication may be reproduced, stored in a retrieval system, or transmitted in any way or by any means, either electronically, mechanically, by photocopy, recording, or any other method, without the prior authorization by the author, except as provided by US copyright law. This book is designed to provide accurate and authoritative information with regard to the subject matter covered. This information is given with the understanding that neither the author, nor Kingdom Being Consultants, LLC, is attempting to render legal or professional advice. The opinions expressed by the author are not necessarily those of Kingdom Being Consultants, LLC.

Copyright 2022 by David Smith
Library of Congress Control Number: 2022909307
ISBN: 9798821884480

Dear Young Reader,

Thank you for your support! I hope that my story helps you to deal with any pain that you are going through.

My goal is to help you to realize that you deserve to be happy. That is why I have written this special book…just for you! I have poured out my heart into these words.

This book is based on things that really happened to me. Please know that if you ever need help, you should go to a mature adult and let them know what's going on. Also, you've always got a friend in me!

Your Friend in Life,

David M. Smith

Dedication

I dedicate this book to God, my family, and any young boy or girl out there who needs to feel loved. We all have a story. Don't be afraid to share yours.

***

Feel free to invite David M. Smith for speaking, teaching, class appearances, conference keynotes, book studies, book signings, and workshops: www.d-m-smith.org

Characters

- David – me
- Mr. Butler
- James Wilkinson
- Anthony
- Angry gang of kids

Table of Contents

Copyright………………………………...	3
Dear Young Reader…………………..	4
Dedication……………………………..	5
Characters………………………………	6
Chapter 1: Trying to Fight the Teacher!...	8
Chapter 2: Anthony the Boxer…….	13
Chapter 3: The "Dark Day"………...	17
Next Time……………………………	22
Questions to Discuss………………..	23

Chapter 1: Trying to Fight the Teacher!

Have you ever felt like life was moving too fast? Like you didn't have enough time to figure just what was going on? I can understand, because that's how I felt! I was losing people I cared about, and it was changing my mood into being angry all the time. This followed me to school and affected my behavior. What I didn't realize was that these things were happening to other kids as well. And it was making them feel the same way as me. This meant that there were a lot of angry kids walking around, and what do you think would happen when they got together? Fights!

Eventually, I had fought almost all the kids in my class, and I wanted a new challenge. That's when I got the dumb idea of trying to take on Mr. Butler! Let me tell you how that went.

"Ok class, settle down. It's time to begin today's lesson," Mr. Butler said to the class. For some reason, that morning I didn't want to be told what to do. "You know what?" I said, interrupting him. "Why don't I teach today? Our first lesson will be how to survive without adults!" Oh, did this make Mr. Butler angry! "David Smith, have you lost your mind? You sit down this instant!" As he said this, he walked over to my desk to stand over me until I listened to him. I didn't like that too much, and a crazy thought came to my mind.

Once he got close enough, I jumped out of my seat really quick and shoved Mr. Butler with all of my might! This was the new challenge I was looking for: trying to fight my teacher! But I had no idea how strong this man was. First of all, my attempt to knock him down was an epic fail. Next, he grabbed me by the collar and lifted me straight up into the air!

I kicked out with my feet and fell to the floor, and that's when Mr. Butler pinned me to the ground. I tried to move and get free, but he was holding onto me tight with his big strong hands. I could still breathe, but it was getting harder and harder for me to break out from under him.

The kids in the class were all shocked to see what was happening! If kids were fighting, you would go and tell the teacher. But what are you supposed to do when the teacher is *in* the fight? I realized that I had bitten off way more than I could chew! Once he knew that I had learned my lesson, he got off of me and let me up. I got back in my seat and didn't look at anyone the rest of the day.

What happened that day didn't stop us from fighting each other, but no one ever challenged Mr. Butler again!

Chapter 2: Anthony the Boxer

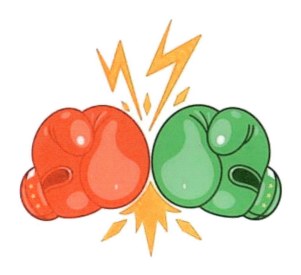

In addition to fighting other kids, I got to see a lot of angry kids fighting each other. One of these fights was between James Wilkinson and a boy named Anthony. At that time, James was walking around acting like he was the toughest kid in class. Anthony had just been moved to our class, and he tried to challenge this "tough kid" right away. "Man, you are *not* that tough! Calm down," he said to James one day.

"And just who do you think you are, newbie?" James said back. "I'm a boxer! I know how to use my knuckles, so you better not try that tough stuff on me!" We didn't believe him, but we had to admit that there were a lot of things different about him.

He was way smarter than the rest of us, and from what he told us, he had a good home life. Both of his parents were there, and they treated him kindly and gave him nice clothes to wear. He seemed to just be violent for no reason. That was actually a scary thought! I kept it in my mind that if we ever fought, I would need to find a weapon.

Anyways, Anthony had challenged James, and a fight was bound to happen! And one day, it did. James decided that it was time to defend his honor, and the two of them prepared for battle. True to his word, Anthony was standing like a boxer, and he fought like one too! "I told you I was a boxer!" he shouted. James was surprised, but he still got a couple hits in. Anthony just had the better fighting skills. It made me wonder if he could have handled Mr. Butler!

We later found out that Anthony's anger came from being made fun of for being a "nerd". So, he studied up on boxing and made it his mission to bust up anyone who called him that! Now I don't remember James ever calling him a nerd, but I guess being bumped down to the problem class made Anthony mad at everybody!

Chapter 3: The "Dark Day"

When it comes to angry kids, there was one day I will never forget. I call it the "dark day", even though the sun was bright and shining at the time. Let me tell you what happened.

Me and two other kids were playing outside by the back gate of the house at 507 Mosher Street. As usual, there were no adults watching us. Normally, we didn't care about this, but on that day, I wish we had someone looking after us.

But it was a calm afternoon, and our guard was down. I don't remember the names of the two kids I was with, because I didn't actually know them. I had only asked them over so that I wasn't totally by myself. Either way, it still didn't stop what happened next.

We were just minding our own business, making up our own games, when we looked up and saw a large group of kids that we didn't know walking up to us. I had this really weird feeling inside telling me that something was up, but I ignored it.

Then as they got closer, I saw that they all had weapons in their hands. Come to find out later that this was a "gang", which is a group of people who are up to no good. Apparently, even kids can form gangs. But you should never join them, because they do bad things to people for no good reason.

This gang of kids had finally reached us, and they had us surrounded. "Um, what's going on?" I asked. But there was no response. They just looked at each other, and then they all shouted, "get 'em!" Before we could do anything, it got crazy! Someone with a metal pipe hit me across my arms, which hurt so bad! I was running and hitting blindly, just trying to bust out of that circle and get away. Finally, there was an opening, and I took off like a jet, running and screaming all the way home!

I had been hit in my funny bone, but there was nothing funny about it! I have no idea what happened to the other two kids I was with, but I do know that the next time I was outside and saw a bunch of strange kids walking up, I got outta there lightning quick!

Most kids who join gangs are angry because of situations at home, and they use violence as a way to express themselves and find relief. But this is not the right way. Hurting other people is never the solution when you feel hurt. At that point, you need to find a healthy outlet, like talking to a friend or doing something good for someone else.

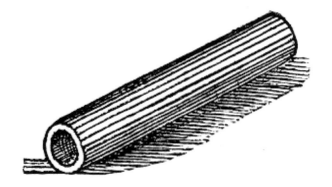

Next Time...

I haven't talked a whole lot about my mother, but stay tuned. She was going through a lot at that time, and I made it my goal to try to protect her as best as I could. That's what I'd like to tell you more about on your next visit. I hope you come back soon! And remember, all of us have a story. Don't be afraid to tell yours!

Questions to Discuss

1. Did David show the proper respect to Mr. Butler?

2. Is it right for a teacher to get physical with a student?

3. How did Anthony feel about being called a nerd?

4. If you get the sense that something bad is about to happen, what should you do?

5. Is it right for kids to form a gang to deal with their anger?

Made in the USA
Columbia, SC
20 November 2024

46773100R00015